Making It!

Business Woman

The **Anaphylaxis** Campaign

Eleanor Archer

W
FRANKLIN WATTS
NEW YORK • LONDON • SYDNEY

Jennifer trained as a nurse but is now a business woman. Her job is to help people give up smoking. She often speaks at medical conferences and appears on television.

Jennifer has a food allergy – she is allergic to peanuts. If she ate a peanut she could have a bad allergic reaction. Jennifer's food allergy doesn't stop her enjoying a busy lifestyle.

If Jennifer ate a peanut her throat would swell up and she would find it hard to breathe. A bad allergic reaction is called anaphylaxis.

3

Today Jennifer is appearing on television.
She has a conference and a meeting to go to as well.
First she gets her son, Alex, ready for school.
"Do you want an orange today?" she asks him.

Alex has food allergies too. He is allergic to nuts and all kinds of pulses.

4

Jennifer puts a snack into her bag. "I might need something to eat later," she thinks. Jennifer doesn't always know where she will be for her next meal.

It's a good idea for people with food allergies to carry a snack as they may not find food they can eat safely while they are out.

5

They set off for Alex's school. "Let's check we have our Epi-pens before we go," says Jennifer. "Then I'll have to rush to get to the television studio."

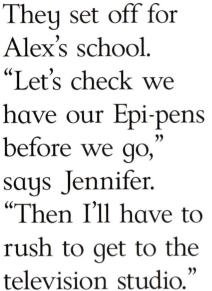

An Epi-pen contains medicine. If a person has a bad allergic reaction, the medicine is injected into them. It may save their life.

At the school Jennifer says goodbye to Alex. "See you later Mum!" he calls.

Alex has an injection kit at school. The adults there know what foods he is allergic to and what to do if he has an allergic reaction.

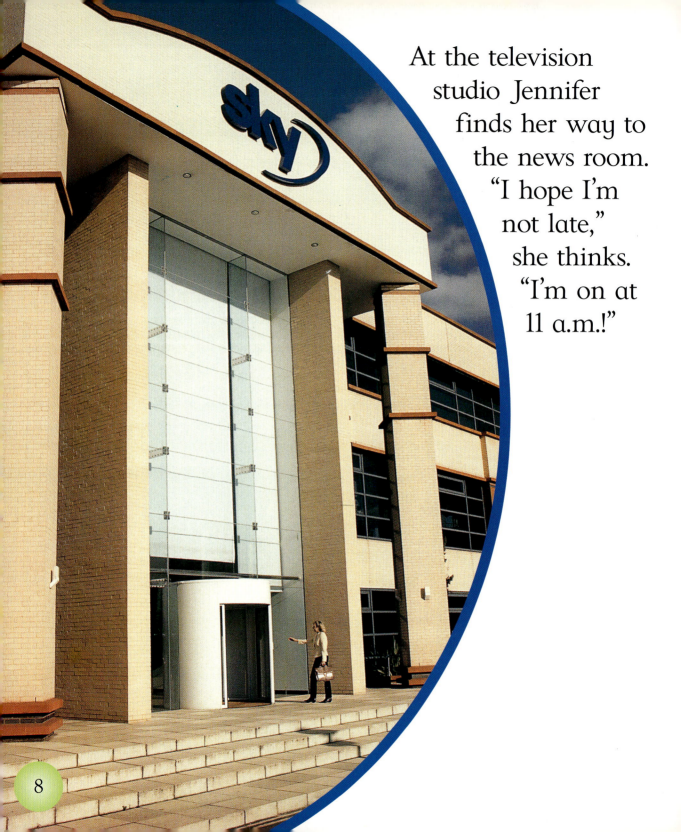

At the television studio Jennifer finds her way to the news room. "I hope I'm not late," she thinks. "I'm on at 11 a.m.!"

Just in time, Jennifer sits
in front of the cameras
with the presenter.
"Can you tell us about
your work?" asks the
presenter. Jennifer
talks to the audience
about how she helps
people to give up smoking.

When the interview is finished,
Jennifer and the presenter relax.
"That was really interesting,"
the presenter says. "Thanks for
coming on the show."

It's 12.30 p.m. so Jennifer goes to a cafe for lunch. She asks if there are any nuts in the sandwich before she buys it.

People who have food allergies have to check carefully that there aren't any nuts in the food they buy.

11

While Jennifer is eating her lunch, her mobile phone rings. "I'll be at the conference at 2 p.m." she tells the caller.

"That was a short break!" Jennifer thinks to herself.

At the conference, Jennifer stands in front
of everyone to talk. She writes important
points on a flipchart. "Any questions?" she asks
at the end.

Later, everyone has a break.
"Would you like a biscuit?"
asks one woman.
"No thanks!" Jennifer says.
"This apple is fine."

There is no box with the biscuits so Jennifer can't check the ingredients. She chooses something she knows she can eat safely.

After the conference Jennifer goes to
her office. She works on her computer.
"I've nearly finished getting my talk
ready for tomorrow," she thinks to herself.

Next Jennifer phones the doctor.
"Good afternoon," she says.
"I'd like to make an appointment
to get a new Epi-pen, please."

At 5 p.m. Jennifer meets a colleague to discuss
what she is doing tomorrow.
"Your talk about the dangers of smoking is
in the afternoon," says the woman.
"That's fine," Jennifer tells her. "I'll see you there."

At last it's time to collect Alex from his after-school club. They go shopping to buy something to eat. "This one says 'May contain nuts'," reads Alex, as they check the labels.

A food label lists the ingredients. It often says if there is any chance a nut, or even a tiny part of one, could be in the food.

It's the end of the day. Jennifer shows Alex
a video of her on television.
"You look really good!" Alex tells his mum.
"Thanks, Alex!" Jennifer laughs.

So you want to be in business?

1. Business includes *many* different types of jobs. When choosing a job, it is *important* that *you* choose something that *you* enjoy doing.

2. Some people work in offices, others work outdoors. Some people travel all over the world for their job. It depends on what type of business you work in.

3. You might need qualifications for the job you want. Find out what subjects you need to study and if there are any exams you need to take.

4. When *you* have decided what business *you* want to be in, see if you can spend some time with people at work. It'll help *you* to find out if *you* would like it or not!

Facts about food allergies

- A nut allergy is one of the most common food allergies. Some people are allergic to pulses which includes peas, beans and lentils.

- Sometimes people are allergic to dairy products (milk, cheese, yogurt and butter) or fish.

- When someone eats something they are allergic to their body reacts badly. Their skin may become red and blotchy and their throat may swell up, making it hard to breathe.

- Some people wear a bracelet which says that they have an allergy.

- An allergic reaction can be treated with the right medicines.

How you can help

- If you are with someone when they have a bad allergic reaction, help them to get their Epi-pen. Tell an adult. Call 999 for an ambulance.

- If you are not sure if a person is having an allergic reaction, you could check to see if they are wearing a special bracelet.

- Remember to think of people with food allergies. Only offer to share food if you know exactly what is in it.

- Make sure you know what to do if someone needs your help in an emergency.

Addresses and further information

The Anaphylaxis Campaign
The Ridges
2 Clockhouse Road
Farnborough
Hampshire GU14 7QY

REACH National Advice Centre for Children with Reading Difficulties
Nine Mile Ride
California Country Park
Finchampstead, RG40 4HT

Food Anaphylactic Children Training and Support (FACTS)
16 Lumeah Avenue
Elanora Heights
New South Wales 2101
Australia

Index

© 2000 Franklin Watts

Franklin Watts
96 Leonard Street
London
EC2A 4XD

Franklin Watts Australia
14 Mars Road
Lane Cove
NSW 2066

ISBN: 0 7496 3667 X

Dewey Decimal Classification Number: 362.4

10 9 8 7 6 5 4 3 2 1

A CIP catalogue record for this book is available from the British Library.

Printed in Malaysia

Consultants: The Anaphylaxis Campaign; Beverley Mathias, REACH.
Editor: Samantha Armstrong
Designer: Louise Snowdon
Photographer: Chris Fairclough
Illustrator: Derek Matthews

With thanks to: Jennifer and Alexander Percival, Sky News, Tesco Stores Plc; The Royal College of Nursing.